RISKY TEXT

Also by
Faroos Omani &
Myla Genéa

Risky & Frisky

Welcome to Risky Text

This book is makes fun of our most interesting form of communication. Texting has turned us into filthy, rude and grammarless animals. Even though we have become savages and lost our love for comma, I personally love nothing more than texting.

All of our jokes are tongue in cheek, light and dark humor with a sprinkle of freak. It's the joy of a good joke, the anxiousness of a vulnerable text with no response and the complete invasion of privacy of texts you'd only send to your lust-buddy.

I hope you enjoy the Risky Text Book and think back to the text you've sent and regretted.

                Welcome to Risky Text

Risky Text

/riskē tekst/

Typing up your true feelings because you want the other person to know how you feel but as soon as you hit the send button, you feel instant regret and/or anxiety until you get a response back

CONTENTS

Preface pg. 6

Mad-Mad pg. 8
*Trying Their Patience pg. 15
*Send Button pg. 23

Only Real Friends 'Get' Us pg. 29
*Reconnecting pg. 41
*Randomness pg. 46

Shooting Your Shot pg. 57
*Indirect Or More Forward pg. 65
*Know It's Not What You Think pg. 84
*Sometimes Failure Makes You Cringe pg. 94

Special Thanks pg. 96

Preface

We wrote this book to show just how funny we have become. In the age of text messages and social media, we have communicated through short-hand, poor grammar and way too many inside jokes.

With 'Risky Texts' we hope start some funny conversations. We also intend to shed light on a few inside jokes as we get closer to answering the best question the 21st century has ever asked

> What have we become?

one last item to note

each thread is rated
by its style of humor
look out for the rating
and beware...

BUT are YOU

MAD

MAD ?

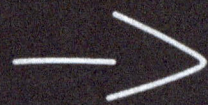

I KNOW YOUR NOT MAD
BUT I'LL PLAY ALONG.

It's rare that anyone is really 'mad' in our little text universe. Most times, if they are 'mad-mad' they'll just stop texting.

Usually, someone else made them mad. They usaully need to hear a good joke, see a good meme and they need something to eat.

If don't believe it, just take a read to see how silly these couples are -when one of them is 'mad-mad'

When you see something on the internet, now you got an attitude

> I decided to make a new email with my middle name and he obviously had problems with it

Mhmm, but you pulled it up. Right, it was like after you decided to tell me and I been seeing it all over, with all these pictures of you over the net. Who are you?

> What are you talking about 🙈 you've known my middle name since last year! you've been seeing my middle name all over?! Really where?

Leave me alone MYLA GENEA at GMAIL

> ahaha okay

Nope, I love you still. I just don't like you 😅

> and why don't you like me 🥴 you need attention

I got so many reasons. Your attention kills pets, burns French toast, and ends up in loud babies*

 #classic #savage #saucy #cringe

sometimes its simple to earn the love back
sometimes it takes a lot more effort
than you thought

If they accept your stank, its real

Leave me alone I'm going back to bed 💩

> Why I don't want to leave you alone (in my cute voice) yea go back to sleep for a bit

I need to eat.

> I understand me too

Okay, find something or find me something*

> I'm searching I found some oatmeal packets, a granola bar, and one Cheerio

One Cheerio 😂 I'm going to hurt you but I want to hug you 😂

> Ahaha come hug me

GOD IS GOOD

> I got into temple!!!

see you were stressing and all worried, but look at that "God is good"

> I KNOW IM SO EXCITED

> NOW I NEED $60 FOR A HOODIE

> PLEASE

Yeah and I said that God is good

> I know, i'm grateful

when I say God is good

you say ALL THE TIME, got damn it

or your not getting the hoodie

 #classic  #savage  #saucy  #cringe

Pick ya battles

I feel like strangling something lol

> Aha why? I don't think you should feel like that on a Saturday night 😂

Cause I'm pissed off lol

> Aha who did it, so i can beat em up

A person lol

> Aww fight a pillow until I get there!!

I can't

ok! then my friend

> Why not?

Somehow that shit would win

> Ahahah wild bull 😂😂

I'm dead ass

...but of course there are other times

when we like to try their patience

Trying her patience

you never want to talk on the phone

> We were on the phone earlier 🙄 but I'll call you once I get home

No I want a phone call right now

> Your 21 now, you don't get to be a brat!

NOW BITCH NOW!!!!

> Nobody is scared of ya lil light skin ass 🥴

you have 5 seconds

> 1,2,3,4

Keep playing!

 #classic  #savage  #saucy  #cringe

someone else

ive met some one else

> What do you mean you met someone else?!!

> Don't fucking play. I will leave my job

> And you don't 'meet' people. You're anti social.

> Do you mean you've been seeing somebody ?!!

Yes and I think he's the one

> HE?!! What are you trying to tell me.

I think I found the barber for the rest of my life

it's A MESS

> ITS EVERYWHERE!!

> I DONT THINK I GET can get IT UP BY MYSELF, when are you coming home?!!

What is it

> im just going to leave it, I have to go, but sure you go straight home

what?!!!

Answer your phone

I'm not going home until I know what you did

 #classic  #savage  #saucy  #cringe

She actually had the nerve to get on a plane

I hope my special dark freak is happier and fuller than a homeless person admitted to old country buffet. I miss you and I love you sweetheart.

> Ahaha yes your freak is feeling extra fed today and slightly tipsy my family is tryna kill me 😂 I miss and love you too baby.

"Baby"? *rolls eyes* I take it back

> Finnnnnneeee Big Head 💁‍♀️

Don't get cute- in another state

Sombody's feeling themselves over there

> Ouuu I haven't gotten that one in a hot lil minute "don't get cute" mmm 🤔 why did I stop 😂

Stop it!!
I will beat you!

 #classic  #savage  #saucy  #cringe

Why she think I'm lying?

you bummass

> Finished a six hour midterm jwnwn it's on and poppin*

Oh word?

> Yeah 😌 We can officially drink and talk about dumb stuff while you act like the girls at onyx

lol whettt u trippen

'Onyx' is one of the most popular strip clubs in the area

> Aha, I'm only serious

U lyinggggg

> Mm-mm

Yea u are

> Aha why do say that?

u be fraudingggg lol

> Look, my phone is on 2% but when I get back it's me and you

yea me and ya hoes

 #classic  #savage  #saucy #cringe

When you trying to push her buttons

Accident 🙈

> so are you going to call me back

Nope 😍

> really.

> you're not going to call me back and say goodnight

So much attitude in such a small message

 #classic  #savage  #saucy  #cringe

Blaming the Send Button

Is one of many ways, we try to apologize for responding to a message hours later. We also blame the send button, or imply that other phone features are the reson communication is so hard.

Honestly, a lot of us are liars. I don't know why it's so hard to say, I don't want to talk to you. But, we know how that special someone gets, when you text slow, or they don't get that 'call back' that you promised several hours ago.

> Damn girly, why doesn't the send button work on my phone?

Umm it work u just don't press it lol

So much love lost...

> Damn girly, why doesn't the send button work on my phone?

Umm it work u just don't press it lol

> Ahaha I'm blaming you

Whatever

> Don't whatever me.

I just did 😭😭😭

> Mhmm keep playing.

Or what??

> *raises eyebrow... You tried it

?? U don't phase me lol

> Aha that's cute

No lil boy

> So anyway, what are we doing this weekend?

 #classic  #savage  #saucy  #cringe

She was serious

Think I'm playing 🔥👌

> Aha 💦 nah we good

Nope 🔥🔥🔥

> Aha oh fuh real

Yea keep playing lol

> Oh I will…

😂😂😂👌👌 say less

What happened to us?

> aha wing it

I am

> sounds like you went from seasonal to part-time

oh I don't do seasonal lol

I should be

Today 1:34pm

wyd

Today 7:08pm

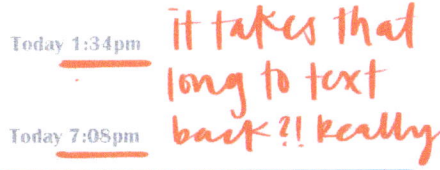

it takes that long to text back?! really

> You and the send button can mix. I'll set it up.

No you and the send button need to talk lol we get a long just fine it be you.

> I thought we took care of us

I guess not

> Mm. did you have a bad day at work today honey? 😂

 #classic  #savage  #saucy #cringe

BRO?! she don't call me bro

Yoooo

Tizzy

Yizzie

> What's up jwnjwn

Idk what's up with u?

You a foul boul lol

> Yo who you talking to?

U bro

You don't answer when I call

ONLY REAL FRIENDS

UNDERSTAND US

Bus drivers are the devil

> Damn bro, the bus did you every type of dirty* I saw you out there gunning.

Lmao. 😂 I kno and I kno that dude saw me too.

U at the stop?

> 😂 No, I'm on the bus

> Ctfu 😂😂😂😂

That's some fucked up shit who was driving?

> You ever see the light skinned driver that looks like spike lee?

yup

Lol he where glasses with a skinny head.

And I be giving that dude fist bumps every day.

> Ahaha no chill, I'll tell him to bring gloves tomorrow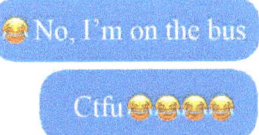

 #classic  #savage  #saucy  #cringe

your friends know how to mess with you

> I was well aware that you were playing geesh who do you think I am 😂?

Ahaha I say *sheesh not 'geesh' Beaker Becky 😂

> I wasn't trying to mimic you I was saying geesh! 😂😂

Say it how I say it punk. 👊🏾

> well you have to be nice if you want me to say it 👊🏾

Ahaha your lil ass don't want any smoke plus I'm the nicest person I know 😂👊🏾

> Who said that!? I'm ready yea mhm 🤭 you have some nice qualities about you 😂 jk yea you're pretty nice peeps

 #classic  #savage  #saucy  #cringe

I care and I won't laugh

> Right I'm showered and I'm clean now you?😊

Eh I'm in my feelings lol

> That's how the best convos get started

lol real wrap?

Ok, but don't crack jokes

> of course not, what's got you in your feelings though?

> This better be a long message

U ever been so hungy but you have no idea what to eat? Lol

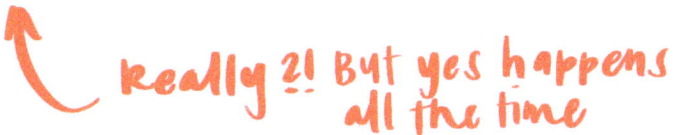
Really ?! But yes happens all the time

Don't be petty and hungry

Good morning

Good morning!!

I want chipotleAnd I'm near on so why not u know

But then my cousin is going to want some, with her broke playing ass

Bitch got money never want to spend it

So are you getting or not

NOO!! I'm not getting it I'll wait

hmm 🫠 you sound like bitch who got money and never want to spend it

I'm blocking you 🫨

Unwanted love

> On my way back home, what are you doing ?

Icing my nose

> Baby you have to stop doing coke

Lol naw

> Aha then what happen

I got this like weird bump under my nostril

> so you got kissed by a mosquito?

Eww no shut up.

but it's more like a hickey than a kiss 😏

> Ahaha ice that lip then love bug

try your luck

> She might let me get it bro

Why you say that

> she said she don't really want to be friends with me

It don't sound like what you think

> Then wish me luck, I'm going to pull up and pull it out on her

Bro, don't do that. The luck I wish for you ain't no good. I never win nothin

> Neither have I, but it's my time

It'll be your time to be register sex offender

Don't do that

 #classic #savage  #saucy  #cringe

Hmmm...

> I'm listening🍗, kills pet,?! pets love me! And my French toast be bomb!

*Burns French toast sticks. I'd love some French toast right now though.

> You can tell me while I'm eating my lunch I'll give you 10 minutes to prep

> its not burned I like mine crunchy

Shady ass, respect the fro

Yaaas witcha Iphone, after I finish paintballing

What?

Disregard that

why she hatin' LMAO

Read 5:34pm

I'm party ready?

That's not what that nappy fro say

shots 🔫👀😭

Lol

I'm blessed and all natural okay!?

 #classic #savage  #saucy #cringe

FRIENDS USUALLY JUST 'GET' US

BUT THEY EASILY FORGET US TOO

RECONNECTING 101

Step 1: Establish contact

Step 2: Check in.

Step 3: Express familiarity.

Step 4: Hit them in the feels.

Step 5: Engage reconnect.

(This is a proven method, that works in the harshes of conditions -yes, it works if you have been out of contact for years. It also works when you someone has a new phone with unsaved numbers.)

*the feels; the emotional hag; be vulnerable or sentimental.

Reconecting 101

Step 1:

> Hey bro

Hey

Step 2:

> How you been

I'm good, how are you?

Step 3:

> We been cool for a while now right?

Of course, what's up

Step 4:

> I need a favor, it's nothing big, I just can't ask anybody else.

umm, tell me what you need first

Step 5:

> New phone who dis? Tell me your name again.

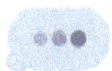

IT WORKS !!!

> Ayo

Sup Moose

> What's going on brobro, I need help with something

What's that • •

> Aha so you're in my phone as 'Guapoe', meanwhile I have no idea who Guapoe

Ctfu whaaaat 😂

> Ahaha 😂 are you laughing at me or my dilemma?

Both?

> Ahaha, chill bigger issues in play, but who am I talking to for the record?

Jasmine weirdo 😂

> Aha 😳hhh, I would have been 😂😂 texted you

Lol smh

 #classic  #savage  #saucy  #cringe

How do you lose a number the same day? playing!

> Ha, I was a film major at Capa, so I'm used to complaining and getting in my critical bag* so to speak. Were you happy to see Will?

Yassss

> Ahaha, simple. He was funny though.

Yea he was chillen

> ???

> ???

Hey who's this?

> Moose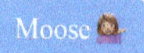

Oh shit! Wassup

Yea to see who number I had put in my notes with no name

A cry for help but you aren't being taken serious

> Mm, wassup then stranger what's poppin*

Nothing much forever Chillen hbu big papa

> Stressin* like fat girls in a line at buffets

Lol why?

> A pimp is overwhelmed, and an og can't have an anxiety attack, I'll lose thug points😂

😂😂😂 I feel u I just gained some points from slapping a hoe for not staying in her lane ya dig?

> Somebody was up trying to get the high score

Lol righttttt

> Naw, forreal though. Im going through something

don't you love when people give in and act as crazy as you are sadly, not everyone will be great with you. In fact, they may stop the randomness immediately

Chef'n evry day all day

> Yo stranger, where are the cookouts at?!👀

Hey, hell if I know. I'm starving myself

> Aha, its really no good out here. Everyone's acting lazy

Basically, you'll have to throw one yourself and invite me

> Ahaha, I whipped out the George Forman what's up?😸

Ayee I'm there lol

> but it only cooks 2 burgers at a time so give me like 3 hours lol

I'll bring me some veggie burgers

Only a few will make sacrifices 4 you

No coffee? How will you survive?

> Aye, I've been wordering the SAME EXACT THING! I'm thinking I'm not going to make it.

*crosses fingers and sacrifices a chicken for you

> Really! Okay hopefully it works!!👌

(Chik fil a) I believe

> in the holy lemondade, I will drink and believe*

All ye of little faith, must not-eth known the taste

> In the order of the nuggets, the fries, and the holy milkshakes

the cashier is my shepard and I shall not want

> ye do I walk through the valley of waffle fries I shall fear no evil,extra sauce is with them

 #classic   #savage  #saucy  #cringe

Awww...

Hey, I just wanted to let you know I was thinking about you we haven't talked in like two weeks or so, but hopefully we can get something to eat and talk. For now though, I appreciate you and I hope nobody is irking you too much right now.

> I got something my eye

Aww it got you tearing up?

> It's the bullshyt on this screen, it's got me cracking up witcho fake nice ass. Lets go to crackerbarrell

Group text stuggles pt.1

Trying to figure out what to do for the weekend

B: sooooo what's going on this weekend

C: It's going to be cloudy with a 10% chance of rain 🙄

A: I'm crying

A: I'm fucking deceased

A: Not deceased 😂😂😂

thanks weather man

C: so drinks and game night?

B: We can play twister lol

B: We trynna feel up on y'all

keep ya hands to ya self

Group text stuggles pt.2

A: Ya'll I hate being poor I'm abou to be a prostitute

> I guess we better make an Instagram page cause I'll be in business witchu

A: 😂😂😂

C: Lord not a prostitute

A: Not today lol I cannot take it *grabs stomach

C: 😊 Be an escort, it's more classy👅👌

⤸ def. a better option
they pay better

Group text struggles pt.3

B: Umm go to K&A Hiring office located inside the evelator to the train

A: Bet I got this y'all wish me luck

K&A is an Area of Northeast Philadelphia with a SERIOUS drug and crime problem

B: tell them I referred you. You'll get a $500 signing bonus and I get $1000 for sending you

A: Oh I'm dead

A referral, always thinking about yourself

he always get something out of it

A: yea escort escort yea that's meeeeee

sketchy uber pt.1

So I caught a uber from the house and this old white man picked me up.. we were having small talk but then he decided to show me how crazy he really was

> aha what did he do?

he started off by making a left, out of the lot instead of a right.

> that's not that weird

it is when every other driver makes a right, but you remember how I was texting you about him then I just stopped for like 30 minutes?

> yeah, I thought your phone died or he took you

He tried and you obviously wasn't trying to save me but I asked him to charge my phone he said 'okay I'll plug it up at the light'

 #classic  #savage  #saucy  #cringe

sketchy uber pt.2

apparently he didn't because I never got a text back he kept looking at my phone and trying to unlock it when i got a message but never plugged it up then he started asking me questions

> lmao wtf like what?

what do you do? I said DDT work
Him: what's that?
Me: I work with patients with mental issues

> you almost got TAKEN what did you do next?!?

then he turned around, looked me in the eye and said 'do you want to help me with mine?'

I was wondering...

> its not that you have random questions it's that you think this is a smooth trantion

Oh I got you lol

Random question, do you take nudes? 🤔

> Of course

> But those are bf privileges 🔐

🤦🤦🤦

SHOOTING YOUR SHOT

The main variation of these three is 'time.' Nothing is more awkward than your friend of fives years hitting you with vulnerable risky text

However, if there's not much of a conversation and someone tries to be confident -saying, I love you, or how's my boyfriend doing? It almost always fails. That's called 'going in hot.' DON'T DO THAt!!

THERE ARE THREE PRIMARAY METHODS OF SHOOTING YOUR SHOT

#1 subtle, which is mixed into conversation, and often goes unnoticed. This is where we people say that want to 'hang' or something, but the other person should get the hint -that it's a date.

> Never heard of that

> Gotta love you

> Is that so 😅

#2 There's the confident approach, where you claim that person early, so they get the hint. We love this one, but sometimes it backfires if you didn't build a relationship first.

> Your bae you know that?

#3 The completely vulnerable approach. This is where people genuinely express their feelings. It's hard not to respect, but this can be hard to handle on the recieving end

> Soo when you first DM me, I forgot what you liike 😅 I saw you and then it all clicked, I remember seeing at the show and thinking you were cute.

Would you have my taken the offer?

When you're trying to ask her out in a subtle way but she ain't feeling it

> You just better drink red wine

I'm more of a Moscato fan

> I figured that's why I said it… you a bum

How?

> Cuz Moscato is for bums

is not

> Can you bowl tho?

Little bit

> How about pool?

Eh not really

> If you can beat me in either one I'll buy you a bottle of Moscato

 #classic #savage  #saucy #cringe

Because why not, right?

> I'm nodding off though pimp ✌️

> I love you

> *the convereation was getting boring*

Moose?

Lol who was that text for?

> 👀 yes? 🤭🤭

??

> That was my cousin playing around

ok lol

Oooo damn...

> How

U crazy

Never heard of that

> Gotta love you

Is that so 🫠

> Yeah lol why that face

Nun 🙈

Gotta love u too

> No I meant that 'you' gotta love 'you' as in I gotta love me

Oooo lol

What didn't you understand?

> Leave me alone.

don't be mean

I miss you

I always say that

> Yeah its your favorite thing to say.

did you mark your calendar for October 13th?

> Yes. I should be in philly. Hopefully.

I hope you will be.

I'm going to hipcityveg.

> Oh, have fun.

I don't want you I just want to hear this story

no you ass. he was a stalker.last weekend. I met a guy in old city. I gave him my number and he followed me. But we got drunk and kissed but now hes sending me pictures

> nice, and really? Did you make a new friend?

eventful

I'm living life.

Next on the agenda is to get with my crush YOU

> out of pocket stories like that don't help your case 😅

I wasn't the stalker I was the victim

> sounds like it was half your fault

maybe it was your fault. If I was over your house that day, I would have never met him

 #classic #savage  #saucy #cringe

Not everybody likes heart eyes as their nicknames

> and met = gave a number and kiss or whatever for you huh?

Lol

Shh

Answer the phone

DUM DUM ANSWER

> you wait until I start doing homework to call me

Don't play with me It's in emergency

BOUL IS CALLING ME

Piece of shit

sent a screenshot of her call log

> I see you removed emojis from my name…

come here and change it back 😈

> doesn't work like that, you can change it or fall back

 #classic #savage #saucy  #cringe

sometimes we get nervous and we are a bit more indirect

other times
we are a lot
more forward
regardless of
anything going
wrong

Sometimes you try it and it works

Yea it's in limerick PA pretty popping u can order food and watch a movie all at the same time

> Aha, do you know where the movie tavern? I heard somethings abou it.

Yea it's pretty fly I've been there a couple times.

> Really?!! That's too cool.

Yea slight work

> Ahaha I see

> 😉 okay pimpin* you've been doing it like that?

Yup what we getting into tonight?

> Depends, do you still have them shorts from way back ?

Of course do you ever think I would throw them away

 #classic  #savage  #saucy  #cringe

Sometimes we miss it

> Lol 😂😂 I need you to answer some questions*

Aha okay ask some questions

> Lol umm why do guys like not care? Like if you don't text them for five hours straight why don't they give af?

Aha sounds like you're texting the wrong people...

> I was talking about you

Ahaha what do you mean

> Nothing

 #classic  #savage #saucy 😬 #cringe

It was 'eww' at first but I want you now...

Heyy

> What do you want.

I want to cuddle

> Eww, no, the best I can do is send a few text with some freaky emojis

> you're the new favorite low-key

I'm the new what?

> 😍😍😍😍😍

> You're bae you know that ?

I like living single, you know that?

 #classic #savage  #saucy  #cringe

How nice is too nice?

> Good morning, for what its worth, I hope you slept well and that the sun peaks in ever so slightly and the birds peck on your window and you sing while you clean up. I wish you a Disney morning, but if it must be some boring day to day monotonous morning may you smile and have the best black coffee in the world. Stretch, smile, and steal the day. Oop I never hit send but gm pimp

Lol thanks

> You're welcome pimpin* I'll bother your crazy self later

Lol wyd?

 #classic  #savage  #saucy

I mean... were still friends though

Lmao some girlfriends 😭 but yes you were def special, you left my ass tho

> 😭 Oh I dang I feel special even though I know I'm special 💁 .. girlfriends ain't been to mommas house but I have *sticks tongue out*

You cut me off

> 😭 I did not, we are still friends and we are taking now

I'm not talking friends mama

Okay, y'all have fun...

let me know about this weekend or something because I'll be free

> Hmm, we'll see. I have plans tomorrow through Friday. But I don't think it's an all day thing 🫣

my friend wants me to fuck her

this weekend

> Okay jwnjwn

but I still want to see you 🥺

> sounds like you'll be busy

so I can be even more busy

> Get your lil freak ass together.

let me show you

Friday night? free crib?

I'm coming back, so I'll be around 🤦🏽‍♀️
would you like to do more?

Maybe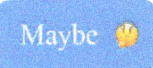

🤭 what would you like to do?

Why you playing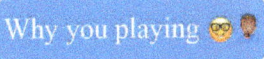

I aint playing boy, what do you wanna do??

Slide in slow 😵‍💫💨 until you tell me its to deep...something of that nature

Nope! Sorry we can't do that 🔴

Saving some for later

Looking like a whole meal ya self 😋

> After dinner we should do dessert 😋

I could've sworn we agreed spontaneous sex was not gonna be our thing

> Sex is always gonna be spontaneous if you ask me 😈

I can't argue with you there 😂

But I'm already in the bed, your dick is good, but not get out of bed good

> Who do you think you are !!

 #classic  #savage #saucy 😬 #cringe

If you go in hot, you could get burned

let me ride you

> Aha this dick is like a medal jwnjwn; it has to be earned 🏆

Being vunlerable, lets see if it lands

Kind of tipsy but can I tell you something crazy?

> Sure

Soo when you first DM me I forgot what you looked like 😂 but I remembered your brand. So I was like ok I'll meet up with him lol. So when I saw you it all clicked, I remembered

> Aha so extra… make me laugh its NOVEMBER!! My birthday month.

Plus I thought you were cute. But then I'm like I do want to work with him so I won't be unprofessional lol.

> Lol I know, thought you were cute too

sometimes the shots land and we realize the chemistry is amazing

then there
are other
times when
you regret it
ever getting
that far

Benefits?

> Oh so friends w/ benefits

Yup. Just like before

> Why do you want me, don't you have someone already?

I do but I like your energy. You're the bougie I need in my life rn lol

If you not with it I get it but I enjoyed your energy

> Um, I'm not. Unless it comes with discounts and a 401k

 #classic  #savage  #saucy

Terrible date pt.1

Bitchhhhh I just remembered he wants to take me out for Valentine's Day

> go girl, get some free love

but I wanted to stay in and watch netflix

and order some wingstop

> lol if you don't get what you want the date can stop, where is he taking you

cheesecake factory

> BITCHH if you don't want to go, send him my number

> take me, tell him it's two for one and if he trynna fuck we gone run!!

lmao you childish. I'mma get ready even though I don't want to

> okay me too lol let me know how it goes

 #classic #savage  #saucy  #cringe

Terrible date pt2

major fail! Not doing that again.. this is the worst Valentine's Day

> what happened

the waitress said he was $7 short.. he left out the house with $40

> Ohhh damn, so I wouldn't have ate

that's not funny

answer your phone

don't be petty, I need to complain over the phone

he apologized and he made me laugh like I'm not mad in the uber. I let him use the bathroom in my dorm, but he's not getting anything else.

he just texted me and said he's still downstairs and doesn't have enough $$$ for a uber. he better call his mama! BITCH ANSWER THE PHONE!!!!

 #classic  #savage  #saucy  #cringe

Remain confident and go for gold

Heyyy sexy

> Yo i sent the wildest text to the wrong person thinking it was you

one what did you send? two who got it?

> when you gonna bust it open, I want to play with it' I sent it to my cousin, and told him I meant the PS4.

Your lying, don't confuse me with your hoes

> lol I don't got hoes

good answer

You don't have to entertain these hoes anymore. Act right and you'll have me. I should be your plan A it would be a sure thing

> lol okay. If you and me tonight are a sure thing, I'll bring a Plan B

 #classic #savage  #saucy  #cringe

What does true love look like?

> I've been relaxing. I found me a sugar-mama and she buys everything I need...

Aye where'd y'all meet?

> We met at Mcdonalds. I was drinking my apple juice and dunking my nuggets like a boss...

Lol oh so u got a Mickey Ds hoe?
That's cool

> No kids and all her teeth, tell me that ain't the lord 😂

Lol nah cuz

U still met her at Mcdonald's

> Ms. Bernadet is not a hoe. She is very nice to me.

If you're not really into someone, how do you tell them?

What if it changes your friendship -what next?

What to do when a 'risky text' goes too far?

The answers is 'it depends.' Not everyone gets 'the hint.' Often times we feel forced to act mean or disappear for good. The next few messages are here for you to reflect -not to judge. I ghost people as often as I visit the dentist lol. I'll learn the right way to do it one day.

Friends for life – no matter what

> Just getting my ego stroked

> Ahah I just wanted to hear your reason, what's my energy like?

From what I remember it was very caring but you have this deep sense of order about you idk how to explain beyond that lol. Like you're sweet but you don't take no shit

> I had fun with you too, you were what I needed 😺👅 and still a really good friend to me that's why I try not to go to long without talking to you!!

Lol what's the kitty and the tongue for ??? ••••

Unfinished business...?

> Finished my last class and got Pizza Hut my food is amazing

Ayeee zaddyyyy

Don't ignore me 🥺

> Right, what's up with zaddy's favorite stripper?

U kno my job is making money

> You better be. I'm almost home though, get your jokes ready so you can make me laugh. 😋

Nope, it was finished

I did feel like we had unfinished business

> 🙍🏾 ouu stop no. I think it was all finished

Ouu excuse me

I gotta put in some more dates downtown again?

> Oh lord! No more dates we are just friends

It's a no for me, but you're still my friend

> Lol yea I don't like to share, you're still my friend though

lol however, I do want a kiss even if it's the last one

Actually no that's not true, can I be completely honest? 🤭

> Of course duh lol

I wanna go on dates, kiss, and occasional make you cum. No strings.

Well I want you to make me cum too.

I don't remember it like that

😂 fair

Lol exactly, I know how to read you 😂
You trying to finesse me like before
just get ya pussy ate and bounce 😂

😂😂 finessing!? I was not doing that and I didn't bounce right after

Lmao yes you did 😂😂😂

No 😂😂 I'm trying to think back on a couple occasions 🤔 I'd cum then we'd kiss, chill, touch, whatever but I wouldn't straight leave after. That's how I remember it 😂🤷‍♀️

Lmao no you left my life 😂

Exactly lmao you'd cum

I'm still here 😂😂.. Yea I'd cum which you wanted me too 😏 and I was always thankful

 #classic #savage  #saucy #cringe

Hm... makes you think

Are you afraid to fall in love?

> I'm afraid of being the only one that falls. While the other one pretends.

I didn't know... okay maybe I did

Lmao you was herrrr

> What you mean I was her? like bae?

yes lol

> Lmao really, why because I went to both houses?

you was bae af

That among the feelings lol

Not many people have ever been to my moms not even gfs haven't 😅😅 not saying I was trying to marry you or something it just shows me I really liked you as a person

Unexpected feelings

We were talking about the past, and what happened to us

I didn't think you were, I know you ain't feeling me no more 😂 nah jk

> Lol we don't speak enough for me to feel you but I could say that you ain't never feel me 😂

What!? 😂 forreal you thought I didn't

> Hell to the no lmao that's why I stopped liking you because I'm like… shes not into me 😂🤷‍♂️

All I can do is laugh 😂😂 because it wasn't like that

> Lol well you didn't tell me you liked me and you kept me at bay 😂🤷‍♂️

Have you ghost-ed someone?

Soo we not friends no more???

Honestly I feel like us having sex ruined our friendship.. we were pretty close

i know... that made me cringe too it's not everyone who deserves to be ghosted but this guy is another story

WOW REALLY.

DAMN.

> Yea I'm bouta get to sleep tho

> Hey just letting you know I'm cancelling the date have a good life it was nice meeting you

U can't accept that I have a daughter.
Fuck u

I'm the realest ni**a u will get

Cuz I have a daughter that's fucked up
I'm to real tfor you

WE HOPE YOU ENJOYED THIS BOOK. WE DEFINITELY GOT SERIOUS IN THE LAST FEW PAGES. IT CAN'T BE ALL JOKES RIGHT? HOPEFULLY, AS TIME GOES ON YOU'LL BE TEXTING RESPONSIBLY. YOU CAN SUBMIT COMMENTS AND YOUR TEXT TIPS TO OUR OUR SOCIAL MEDIA HANDLES AT ANY TIME. WE ALL HAVE TO GET BETTER AT SENDING RISKY TEXT.

SINCE YOU MADE IT THIS FAR YOU DESERVE SOMETHING RIGHT? OR IF YOU DON'T WANT IT, YOU CAN CLOSE THE BOOK NOW. WE ADDED A TINY SECTION OF OUR TEXT LINGO DICTIONARY (COMING SOON).

NOW THERE ARE A FEW MORE 'RACEY' TEXT BEYOND THIS PAGE. YOU MAY NOT LIKE WHAT YOU SEE -BUT IF YOU JUST WANT TO LOOK, THE 'BETWEEN US' PORTION OF THIS BOOK IS DEDICATED TO UNFILTERED COUPLES.

EMOJI BASICS

 = drip; used when commenting on something stylish, to have sauce or a unique quality.

splash; a verb referring to a very fun and adult activity if she has the super soaker, bring a towel.

 = This emoji is oftern used in combination with other emojis or suggestive text messages., because it has an air of 'because I said so' and a sprinkle of 'I want you'

 = no cap; a phrase of endearment meaning, 'I am not lying.' 'I am not exaggerating.'

The peach; a delectibly juicy and wonderful fruit

 = Also used when referring to 'the booty.' The 'Geogia Peach' is an inside joke referring to what you would see in most any Atlanta Strip club.

 = The eggplant; an underappreciated vegetable with a weird taste.

More commonly, this emoji is used in place of the male estrimety.

RISKY TEXT LINGO*

Jwnjwn
/jônjôn/
Noun
Originated in Philadelphia, can be refer to a person (mainly female)

Personal
/ˈpərs(ə)n(ə)l/
Adjective
Someone who you would do anything for because they are special to you

Finessing
/fəˈnes/
Verb
Avoiding a situation or trying to get more out of the situations by playing or trying to avoid a person

Out of pocket
/out-ēv-päkēt/
To describe someone who is rude or a person who came at you the wrong way

You playing
/yoo,yə- plā/
To describe someone who is always avoiding something or giving someone the run around

Thirsty
/ ˈTHərstē/
Not taking no for answer; an attention getter, doing anything to be noticed

Boul
/bull/
To describe another male and sometimes female in philly

Simple
/simpəl/
To describe one who is silly or someone who acts like an airhead at times

Freak
/ frēk/
Referring a woman or man who is very sexual and likes to do kinky stuff

99

SOME THINGS STAY

BETWEEN US

Picking petnames

> Good morning love, I hope you have a wonderful day…

> Good morning to you too boo, I hope you're having a good day as well

> Ooo, no 'boo' pick another one ponyboy

> Aha.. honeybun, hun, sweetie, favorite aha?

> umm, I'll let 'love' slide for now

> ahaha mk Amore

If your not ready to send risky texts, make em wait

I'm tryna make this money for the rent

> Aha get a part time Splenda-daddy

byeeee like

> Aha why do I like messing with you?

Idk but forreal where my cut zaddddyyyy 🤤

> Aha you play 😏

You zaddyyyyy

> Ahaha oh I'm zaddyy now

> Aha okay zaddy got some words for you then

Waiting

If you go in hot, it gets hotter

Lmao yeah you a whole snack from the baby hairs and eyes

> I'm a whole meal, eat up

Girl don't talk to me like that

I will fuck the shit out of you no bs 😂

> Okay 🙊 I'll keep my thoughts to myself lol

Lol no don't

it's better when you tell me things like that 🤭

There's always time to be freaky

We were talking about eating healthier and working out

> we are.. 'But you have a plan A and a sure thing' baby girl remember that 😉 but all you have do is hit the grocery store and take test yo 😂

gotcha ya like you don't stay at shoprite 😅 I'm the errand runner in the house what can I say

> I go I don't live there, but that's cute

Want me to be your personal trainer

> Nah, just back that ass up and you'll be all the workout I need #savage

She was going away on a trip

Ha, I can't have you walking around in another state needing a fix...

> Ooo! You're hilarious I know how to control myself honeybun no worries

Yeah okay "honeybun" don't get addicted...

> And why you acting like we won't be on FaceTime 👅

> Whateva can't I just like you and the sex just be a bonus sheesh, like I'm going to miss giving you awkward hugs when I'm gone

I'll let you give me an awkward hug before you leave.

> Oh! Thanks for giving me permission means a lot.

We got thangs to do when I get off this plane

Aha goodbye, bring my pussy back safe

*like you're supposed too

> Stay busy, What are you doing? I'm horny when I get back f*ck me outside in the park

> and everywhere else

> I'll bring it back safe and soaking

you can look don't touch

ITS BEAUTIFUL!!!

I wanna play in it

> Thank you, you can look at it 😂

Lmao excuse meeee, I'll keep that in mind if you try to touch my hair too

> I'm good 😂

Don't Play

> Daddy will not be babying you anymore… just keep me sexy and I'll try to fight em off

Oh really mmm… Daddy do better than 'try' so you can stay sexy

>  Mm

Hinting at an appointment*

> No I got some booty shorts instead to add to my collection

Aha you and these lil booty shorts… remind me to get some monopoly money to tuck in nem tings*

> Yea I won't let you forget

Yaaas Freak

> 👅 aha what are you up too

Mm, put that tongue away before you start something 😉 I'm reading now.

> Aha mk I'll save it for later 😴 me too this bio book is putting me to sleep

Get through it girl. I might come visit you tomorrow and brighten up your lil break between classes

 #classic #savage  #saucy #cringe

Ask for more, you just might get it

> come thru.. you know we got things to do

And eat

> You want pancakes?

Mm, yeah plus…

> Strawberries? Sweet tea? This jolly mouth?

Okay freak 😂

Don't cancel sex appointments!

Aha goodbye, here's the love 🥰😍

> I'll be happy with this for now.. but Tuesday you'll have to amp it up

bad news*

> What happen

The Freak Week tour* might be canceled.

> FOR WHY?! NO IT'S NOT!! MAKE IT HAPPEN, I've been gone for 2 weeks

> ANSWER YOUR PHONE RIGHT NOW!!!

 #classic  #savage  #saucy 😬 #cringe

Gimme More

> He nearly drank all of my tea! That mix was really good and it was sweet enough too

I just tasted it. It is pretty good. Can't have anything nice

> Yes it was delicious! I wish I had more

Thirsty ass come get some beecho americano

'Beecho' refers to the male extremity. 'Americano' refers to a coffee (expresso) based beverage. Thus, he meant oral yuck-yuck.

>  bring it to me

It'll be right up at the bar (coffee shop counter)

> No it will not! You can't be letting people see what I got

They're always nastier than you thought

That's a 'you' job right there…

> 😂😂 it's a me job!? I keep you alive.. you keep me alive and we try our best to stay alive

You want to suck me dry and take me out- I'm just taking you with me.

> Yes I do, I mean you could lick me dry so we'll be even 👅😋

So you have been drinking*

> Ahaha I'm only nasty when I drink?

You're nasty every time I talk to you…

> How it should be and how you like it, so sounds good

Mhmm, so you're having fun out there?

The quiet girls are always the nastiest

Oh, well hi stranger since you never came to see me.

> Whatever like you didn't see me everyday or sit next to me on occasion

I sat next to you because somebody stole my seat cornball 😉

> Mhm whatever you say.. "you aint got to lie"

Aha you're right, the pancake was jiggling. I just had to come see if you were free balling.

> no the cake just a lot of jiggle ahaha!

Aha girl, so anyway What are we doing over there ?

> you don't have to believe me its cool

 #classic  #savage  #saucy #cringe

THE END

www.ingramcontent.com/pod-product-compliance
Lightning Source LLC
Chambersburg PA
CBHW061233070526
44584CB00030B/4106